# When We Walk With The Lord

**By Teus and Maria Kappers**

**Mill Lake Books**

Published by Mill Lake Books
https://jamescoggins.wordpress.com/mill-lake-books/

Cover design by Dean Tjepkema

ISBN: 978-1-7771926-2-4

# Dedication

This is the story of Teus and Maria Kappers and how God brought them together from different countries so that they could serve the Lord together and prove how great and trustworthy God is.

This testimony is dedicated to our three children, our five grandchildren, and those great-grandchildren yet to be born so that they might set their hope in God (Psalm 78:6-7).
"I have called you by name; you are Mine!"
(Isaiah 43:1)

# Table of Contents

# Foreword

"Those who go down to the sea in ships, who do business on great waters; they have seen the works of the Lord" (Psalm 107:23).

It is my privilege to write a Foreword for a book telling stories of God's amazing grace and how that grace was shown to seafarers of the world.

From the time Teus and Maria trusted Jesus Christ as their Saviour, they understood that they were in the service of the Most High God, the Creator, the Redeemer, the King of Kings, the owner of the cattle on a thousand hills, the One who is omniscient, omnipotent, and omnipresent. They wanted to serve Him, and this gave them the courage to take steps of faith that would have made most of us cower away in unbelief. They put their trust in Him, blind to the naysayers and blind to the threats. Praying and putting their trust in the Lord, they moved forward as He opened doors and led them.

Teus and Maria are examples of what God can do when we truly believe in Him. That is why I know you will enjoy reading this book. In it, you will see the hand of God work through two everyday people.

Teus and Maria are entrepreneurs, visionaries. Part of their vision was that the work they were doing would continue long after they were not able to do it themselves. Wisely, they gathered a group of people to share the vision of taking the gospel to the seafarers coming to the port of Vancouver. These people became partners in the work of the Lord done through Lighthouse Harbour Ministries, and we pray this ministry continues sharing the gospel until the Lord's return.

Teus and Maria did not write this book to bring attention to themselves but to bring glory to God. They wanted to share with their children, grandchildren, and future generations of their family, as well as others, what the Lord has done and can do. Their attitude is summed up in Psalm 115:1: "Not to us, O Lord, not to us, but to Your name give glory, because of Your lovingkindness, because of Your truth." Teus and Maria faced many trials along the way, and I am sure there were times when their faith was stretched to the point that they thought it would break. But I believe they are going to hear: "Well done, good and faithful slave. You were faithful with a few things, I will put you in charge of many things; enter into the joy of your master" (Matthew 25:21).

Teus and Maria, thank you for the godly examples of living for the Lord that you have been to me and to so many others. May the Lord continue to bless you as you serve the greatest Master of all.

Loving regards,
Ray Hanna,
Senior Chaplain,
Lighthouse Harbour Ministries

"Tell of His glory among the nations, His marvelous deeds among all the peoples" (Psalm 96:3).

# 1
# Teus: Dutch Roots

I (Teus) was born on August 29, 1950, a few years after the Second World War, in the small town of Harderwijk in central Holland, a town famous for its smoked eel. I was the third of four children. My father worked in insurance and market gardening. Our home was small but cozy and was at the edge of the old town, which dated back to 1252 AD. It was then located on the Zuiderzee, now called Veluwemeer (Lake Veluwe) because dikes were later erected to create more farmland, cutting our town off from the open ocean.

Our parents loved us and gave us a rich family life with strong family traditions. Outside the family, our life revolved around our church and other nearby families. We would attend services at the Reformed church each Sunday morning and most Sunday evenings. My father would give thanks to the Lord before and after each meal and would read a portion of Scripture. As we grew older, he would ask one of us children to say grace, which would make me feel very uncomfortable.

The earliest church service I remember was in 1962. The church members were called together for a special meeting to pray because a third world war was a real possibility. It was the time of the Cuban missile crisis, and the nuclear bombs that had been dropped on Hiroshima and Nagasaki, Japan were fresh in everyone's minds. Next to me in the church pew stood a little old lady, dressed in traditional black clothing. Big tears were running down her wrinkled face as we sang together, "Nearer, my God, to Thee." The huge pipe organ made the old hymn sound even more dramatic. The church was packed. God answered prayer, and a nuclear war was averted as Nikita Khrushchev and John F. Kennedy reached an agreement.

Growing up in my town was wonderful. We could choose our playground, and every day it was somewhere else—on the lake, in the forest, or in the wide farm fields. As children, we were forever digging in the soil outside our home and coming across skulls and bones and other artifacts from centuries ago, which held no value to us. Our bikes were our primary mode of transport. There are more bikes than people in Holland. At one point, I had three. My grandmother was still riding on a bike at age 80. Cycling in Holland is easy, as most of the country is as flat as a pancake.

## A Great-Great-Great-Grandfather

Later in life, when the internet was developed, I learned an interesting story from an uncle who had researched our family tree (on my mother's side). Some of my Juch ancestors had immigrated to Holland from Germany. One member of the family had an interesting testimony. Johan was born in 1819 and, after completing school, started work in a shipyard in Den Helder in the north of Holland. This was the place where the Lord started to work in his heart and he was saved. At age 21, he joined a church group named "Under the Cross." As he grew in the Spirit and experience, he became a pastor in this denomination. Because of eye trouble, he went to an eye doctor for treatment. Something went wrong, and he became totally blind. From then on, he was called "The Blind Shepherd." He became dependent on his son to read for him and to guide him from place to place. In those days, there were no seeing eye dogs. Johan continued to have a real heart to serve the Lord and a heart full of compassion for souls. On one occasion, he wrote a letter to the then king of the Netherlands, William III, concerning the well-being of his soul. This letter moved the king, and he invited Johan to come and preach at his palace, which he did. As a result, the king recommended he visit his eye specialist in Belgium at his expense. He went, but it did not help, and he remained blind for the rest of his life.

## Life Change

In the late 1960s, life seemed to change. Church lost its attraction. It was the time of the Beatles, and music tastes changed. Motor bikes and cars became available and changed our pace of life. We now had easy access to the big cities, and drugs were starting to change the lives of some of my school friends. At a business school in the town of Amersfoort, I was offered LSD. Looking at the condition of my friend—he was acting like a zombie or someone from another planet—the idea of taking drugs did not attract me. But I started to think about the purpose of my life. Why was I here? What was the point of it all? Was there anything worth living for that would endure past this present life?

At that time, my ambition was to become a sales rep for a business. My particular interest was in the catering industry, as I had already worked in a local bakery. I was still too young for this, and I also had a legal obligation to serve in the Dutch army for 18 months. I put in a request to join the military police in the country of Suriname, which had been a Dutch colony. I passed all my tests and exams and was accepted, partly because I am 201 centimetres (six foot, seven inches) tall and they liked big guys like me. Disappointment came a few weeks later when early one morning I received a letter from the Ministry of Defence saying that because of a surplus of men (due to the large number of Baby Boomers) my name had been selected at random and I was excused from joining the military. What now? What should I do?

My parents had started a flower shop, and they were keen for me to join them full-time in the business, but that was not what I really wanted.

## A Very Special Night

Not long after this, on April 5, 1970, I was watching TV in a small corner of our living room. The TV was showing a program about a Billy Graham crusade in Europe (Euro 70). Billy Graham was being interviewed, and he gave the most interesting answers—about what it means to be a Christian and how to be saved. Of course, I believed I was born a Christian, but he explained that we have to be born again, as Jesus said. So far, I had lived a very self-righteous life. I had observed drug people and thought, "Not me." Some of my colleagues and I had been in the "red light district" in Amsterdam, and I had thought, "I am glad I am not like them." But deep down in my heart I knew I, too, had sin and needed to repent. That night, when I went upstairs to my bedroom, I knelt down and asked the Saviour to forgive me and come into my heart. After this prayer from my heart, my life has never been the same! I experienced what the hymn says: "O the deep, deep love of Jesus, vast, unmeasured, boundless, free, rolling as a mighty ocean in its fullness over me."

The next day, I told my parents what had happened. They were totally puzzled, as they had never seen me as being that religious. "You'd better see the pastor," they said. "He will be able to help you."

So I made an appointment to see the pastor a few days later. His advice was: "Don't worry. You will get over it. See me again in a few weeks' time when you will feel better." I felt deflated. This man, who stood in the pulpit of our church every week, did not have one word of encouragement for my newfound spiritual life with my Saviour.

The next couple of weeks went by very fast. I started reading the Bible by myself and praying on my own. On one of these occasions, it was as if the Lord spoke to me clearly: "I want you to become a missionary." I became very excited, but I had no idea how I should go about doing this.

Behind our home lived a couple who had just returned on furlough from mission work in Brazil. In their window was a small poster advertising the Billy Graham crusade in Germany on TV. I took the courage to ring their doorbell and ask them about the poster. They were very friendly and invited me in. I explained my situation and my experience. They were happy to hear what I had to say and encouraged me to go on trusting the Lord for my future. They were the first people who had ever prayed with me. When I told them that God had spoken to me regarding missions, they recommended that I seek help from a man who lived down the road from us. They said, "He knows a lot about missions, and he will be able to give you advice."

So, a day later in the evening, I knocked at the door of Anne van der Bijl. I had never met him before, but I explained who had sent me to him. That seemed to do the trick, and he let me into his home. The reason for his suspicion was understandable, as later I found out that this man was "Brother Andrew," a man known around the world and the author of the best seller *God's Smuggler*. I had never heard of him or of the organization he had founded, Open Doors, or that he had been smuggling Bibles into Eastern Europe. After I explained the purpose for my visit, he strongly advised me to go to a Bible college to study in preparation for the mission field. I had never heard about Bible colleges or where they were and how to get there. Brother Andrew gave me a sheet of paper with a list of such colleges all over the world. "Just write to them and ask if you can come to study," he suggested.

After I got home that night, I had a look at the list of colleges more closely. It suddenly dawned on me that if I would take this next step, what would happen to the sailing boat I was planning to buy? Would I have to give up this idea?

Back to the pastor of my church I went. I think he was surprised to see me again. He had probably been hoping that my newfound faith was not going to last. When I told him that my next step in life was to become a missionary, he was astounded. "What!?" he said. "Do you know that missions don't pay very well and it will really upset your parents if you leave them?" (He was right about the latter. It did upset my parents.) I don't know where I got the courage to ask the pastor: "But did you become a pastor because of money?" His response shocked me. He said, "Yes." He made no mention of God's call on his life. That was the last time I ever met that pastor. I realized that from that time on I had to fellowship with real believers who could help me in my next step of faith. God provided, as I got to meet many staff of the Open Doors organization and other missionaries.

One evening when I was home alone, I took out the paper that Brother Andrew had given me and looked over the addresses on it. There were places all over the world, and I was confused about which one to apply to. So, I simply prayed and closed my eyes and let my finger drop onto the paper. It came down on the Bible College of Wales in Swansea in the United Kingdom. I had to look on a map to see where this city was. (This was in 1970, before the days of the internet.) So I wrote a short letter of application with my personal testimony and the name of the person who had recommended that I apply.

The whole process created great tension between my parents and me, but I knew it was the right decision to make even if it upset my parents and many others. But it hurt. I tried to reason with them, pointing out that if I had been in the army, I would have been away for two years, and that would have made them proud as I would have been serving the country. But leaving for missions? And not knowing where it would take me?

My bakery boss added his bit of advice: "You realize that when you leave, I will not continue to pay you? Do you think that the ravens of Elijah are still alive to bring you food? They won't be bringing you food from this bakery." Now, fifty years later, I can testify that those ravens are long dead, and my bakery boss is too, but the God who sent those ravens is alive and well, and He has never failed to supply my needs and more. My wife and I often say, "God spoils us because He loves us" and "The earth is the Lord's and all it contains" (Psalm 24:1).

I know that all of these struggles were spiritual battles. The enemy was trying to stop me from doing God's will and fulfilling His purpose in my life.

In early August 1970, a letter from the Bible college came in the mail saying, "After prayerful consideration, we have accepted your application. Please come." About six weeks later, I was on the Hoek van Holland night ferry to Harwich, England, together with another Dutch student.

Earlier that evening, after supper, my father had read the Scriptures, and in the middle of his reading, he had broken down in tears because I was leaving. This was the first time I had ever seen my father cry. I was embarrassed and had no words of comfort. Now I know why he cried—it was because he loved me!

After a long, nine-hour ferry journey and a train trip to London, we arrived in the big city. Then we crossed London in a taxi to get to the British Rail station for another four-hour ride to Swansea, Wales. It was all a little hard to take in. The college grounds and buildings looked impressive, and I was assigned a room in the men's building. My roommate was a man named David, from Nigeria. He was incredibly homesick for his wife. His English was perfect, but mine was not, indeed far from it. I discovered that my school English was of little help. I knew little beyond "yes" and "no." But I was sure I would learn.

A few days before I had left Holland, I had taken a Dutch lady to the airport in Amsterdam. She, too, was going out to be a missionary, in Brazil. During our trip, she told me that while she had been taking nursing training in London she had met a wonderful girl from Germany who was serving as a midwife in east London. She suggested that Maria would make a very good wife for me. But that was not the reason why I was going to Bible college, and marriage was the last thing on my mind. Anyway, the rules of college were very strict. There was to be no talking between men and women. Yet, on our first night of student introductions, I met Maria for the first time. The rest of the story is for another chapter.

# 2

# Maria: The Story of a German Family

## by Maria Kappers

A man by the name of Gerhard Meltzer was living in a beautiful city called Schwerin in the province of Mecklenburg, Germany. He came from a family of Lutheran pastors, and his father was a pastor at the big cathedral in Schwerin called the Schweriner Dome. But Gerhard was a grain merchant and worked with many Jewish businessmen. One day, Gerhard met a beautiful young lady named Maria, the only daughter of a cloth merchant. Gerhard and Maria were married a year later when he was twenty-two and she was only nineteen. At twenty, Maria had her first son, Eberhard. Ten years later, a second son was born, and they called him Klaus.

Toward the end of the Second World War, the state police came to the house and took Eberhard to become a soldier. He was only seventeen. If he had not obeyed, they would have shot him at the door. A few months later, Gerhard and Maria received the news that their son had been killed in Russia. The grief, especially for Maria, was unbearable.

Then, on December 22, 1945, a little girl was born—me. I was very premature and only weighed four pounds. My mother, after whom I was named, was very sick following the birth, and they thought she was going to die. It was at the end of the war, our country had lost everything to the communists, and incubators were not available. In order to help me survive, they put me between two hot water bottles. By God's grace, we both survived. I grew up but always remained very petite

The Russians had taken the town and destroyed much of the castle. They also took people's houses and their businesses, so the people who had at one time been wealthy were now very poor. Four other families were moved into our home, along with a house leader, so we were not even in charge of our own home anymore.

During that very stressful time, Gerhard became sick and had to go to the hospital in Leipzig. My mother rented a room, and I, at four years old, went with her, while my brother Klaus had to stay with friends in Schwerin. My father was in hospital for one and a half years and lost seven of his ribs, which had to be removed for the lung surgery. There were no antibiotics in East Germany. My father had a brother in West Germany who was a medical doctor, and after a while he was able to send us penicillin. My uncle had been in the war as a medical doctor, had been captured by the French, and after the war had stayed in the West rather than returning to East Germany.

After eighteen months, my father was finally released from hospital, but he could never work again. He had lost one lung because of the terrible infection he had had. When we came back to Schwerin, Gerhard and Maria realized that they could not stay in a communist country, where there would be no future for their children. My brother already had started to learn Russian at school, and church life was made difficult as communists did not believe in God. My father requested permission for the whole family to move, and the request was granted. The authorities said he would be worthless to society and we could go.

## Moving to the West

In 1952, our family moved to the small village of Besenfeld in the Black Forest. At that time, the total population was 500. We rented an apartment above a stable full of cows and horses, but all the old, big furniture my parents had brought with them fit in. Our neighbours were all farmers, and they spoke a dialect which we could not understand. I was six years old and seemed to learn the dialect quickly, but not my parents. They forever struggled with it.

For me, school started in the spring. The winter had been bitterly cold and long—it was the Black Forest, and the elevation was about 800 metres. Our school was small, and grades 1-4 were all in one room.

My best friend was named Annerose, and we are still friends today. She lived right opposite me, and at night we could look out our bedroom windows and talk. She had two sisters and one brother. Since Annerose was the oldest, she had to help a lot on the farm and in the home, and as I grew up, I tried to help her with whatever I could. My brother had left home to study to become an engineer, and he came home seldom, only during breaks in the school year.

When it was time to bring in the potato crop, I also would help in the field. As long as Annerose and I could be together, we had lots of fun. We would throw the tiniest potatoes at each other and show off who had the dirtiest hands. At the end of our work, Annerose's parents would make a bonfire, throw some potatoes into it, and let them cook, dirt and all. When they were done, we would carefully peel off the dirt and skin and eat them. Of course, our mouth was totally black, but that was the fun of it.

One day, Annerose's mother had made a blueberry cake, and we found out that it was stored in the pantry. We got a knife, went down to the pantry, sat down, and ate three-quarters of the cake. It was yummy! Annerose's mother was not amused.

Every time I went to play with my friend, my clothes would end up smelling like a cow stable. My mother was not exactly pleased. We had no shower or bath in the house, so my mother and I would go once a week to a shower house, usually on a Saturday so as to be clean for Sunday. The rest of the week we would wash in the kitchen sink with warm water. The toilet was something else. It was made out of red clay and had no flushing water. Everything went straight down to the stable. One day as I sat there, I heard a voice from the courtyard between Annerose's house and ours. I decided to climb up onto the toilet and see what was going on. All of a sudden, I and the toilet came crashing down. The clay was old and not very strong anymore, and the toilet had broken into many pieces. My father was reading the paper and heard the crash. It was not easy to tell him why this had happened. He was not amused for sure. However, he put all of the pieces on our dining room table with lots of newspaper underneath. Then he cleaned it and used UHU, a very good German glue, to put it all back together again. For about a week, we had to use the old-fashioned pot.

In spite of all this, my childhood was really wonderful and carefree. We could play in the forest alone and pick lots of blueberries and wild raspberries, which my mother would turn into delicious jam or juice for the winter. We had no freezer, so everything had to be boiled and preserved.

Every Sunday, we would put on our Sunday clothes and go to the local Lutheran church. In the afternoon, I would go to a Methodist church for Sunday school, where we were required to learn Bible verses. The people there were very kind, and all the children would get a chocolate before we went home.

But all good things come an end. After grade 5, I had to start high school. I had to be on the bus by 7:00 a.m. as school started at 8.30 a.m. I had to be up early so my mother could put my hair into waist-long braids. High school was a different life altogether. After a year, my parents felt for my sake that it would be better to move nearer the school, so we moved to a town called Freudenstadt, which means "Town of joy." Why did it have that name? During the 1600s, there were a group of people in France who believed in salvation by grace and not by works, following the teaching of John Calvin. These believers, called Huguenots, were being persecuted by the Catholics, and the ruler of Freudenstadt opened the door to these Huguenots to come and live in safety. Freudenstadt is a beautiful town, although it had been burned to the ground twice. Whenever the townspeople rebuilt, they always started with the church and the houses around it. For my parents, this town was wonderful, as there were concerts to go to and other cultural opportunities, things which they had used to enjoy during their earlier years in Schwerin.

One summer during our time in Freudenstadt, my parents sent me to a Bible camp run by Protestant sisters called Aidlinger Schwestern. We went to a lake called Titisee. It was very beautiful, we learned much about the Bible, and we were invited to sit down with one of the sisters and talk about our faith. As teenage girls, we felt very much loved and accepted just as we were. One evening, I went to one of the sisters and told her I wanted to accept the Lord Jesus as my Saviour. She was very thrilled to hear that. She prayed with me and gave me a verse from Isaiah 43:1: "Do not fear, for I have redeemed you; I have called you by name; you are Mine!" That was my first step with the Lord Jesus. When I went home and told my parents, they did not quite understand. I had been baptized as a baby, and the Lutherans teach that that makes you a Christian. However, I must say that my parents were deeply God-fearing people. On Good Friday, my parents would dress up in black to go to communion. My father would say, "This is the darkest day the world has ever seen. God's own Son laid down his life for the whole world so that there would be forgiveness of sins for all who put their trust in Him." From that summer, I had a new life and a personal relationship with the Lord Jesus.

After high school, I went for one year as a nanny to France, to a beautiful place in the south where there were lots of lavender fields. I was with a doctor's family which included two boys and two girls. I had been warned by the previous nanny that I might find a frog or a snake in my bed. The youngest boy loved animals, and one day he rescued an owl with a broken wing. It was still young, so we fed it bits of liver and chicken. It recovered, and when it was strong enough, we let it go from the balcony. The next day, the whole owl family sat on the balcony as if to say, "Thank you." I would go out on long bike rides in the country, and one afternoon when I came home, Pierre, the youngest, had laid out a snake in the garage. Fortunately, it was dead, so I thought now was my chance to be brave. I admired the snake, then slowly picked it up and put it around my wrist like a bracelet, and said, "This is very pretty." Fortunately, I never found a snake in my bed.

After my time in France, I came home to Germany and entered nursing school for three years. For two years, I was in a small, old town called Herrenberg, and one year I spent in Stuttgart. During my final year in nursing, my father passed away of a stroke followed by a heart attack. You can imagine how hard this was for my mother, with no one living at home with her anymore.

During my nursing training, the Lord spoke very clearly to me about becoming a missionary. I made enquiries in Tubingen and was told I should go to Britain and do my nursing training over again, as the British RN degree is accepted all over the world. I prayed much about this and was particularly concerned about who would look after my mother. Then I read Matthew 10:37: "The one who loves father or mother more than Me is not worthy of Me." So, I went to my mother and explained everything to her. She was very gracious and understood. Before leaving, I helped her move into a smaller apartment, which was very nice, with a small balcony and within walking distance to the shops and the church. In the building were some other kind ladies who befriended her.

**On to Britain**

I found work again as a nanny to an English family in order to learn the language better. I took my first airplane flight from Stuttgart to London. The lady could not be at the airport to pick me up as she had three small children, so I had been told to take a taxi. I spoke hardly any English, but the taxi driver spoke French, in which I was fluent. He told me that it was rush hour in London and it would be too difficult to get through, so he took me to a café. My mother had bought me a brown suit with a little fur collar, gloves, shoes with high heels, and a big hat. I looked like a true lady and felt I could have played in *My Fair Lady*. We drank our tea, and he paid for me, and then we went to the appointed place in Hammersmith, an upper-class area. He knocked at the door for me, and when Mrs. Makower opened the door and paid the taxi fare, he told her that I was a bit nervous (which was true).

The family were very kind and welcomed me into their home. They had three children, ages five, three, and one. The mother had chosen to bring the children up the Dr. Spock way, with no discipline at all. That is why a nanny had been hired to come in and clean up the mess.

The parents were believers and went to a local evangelical Anglican church. Twice a week, I went to English classes to learn proper English. For me, I found it was best to live with the people and learn the language that way. During the week, I was invited to a Bible study, and soon they asked me to join them for services in a hospital and a seniors' home. God truly had His hand upon me, providing Christians to help me all along my way. London is a very large city with many temptations, but it was as if the Lord was saying, "You choose to follow Me, or you will end up down in the gutter in London."

One Sunday, a missionary came to visit our church and speak about his work in Africa. He was German. I spoke with him after the service, and he told me I could come to Leicester to do my nursing there. He and his wife had come back for the sake of their two children's education. So, after one year in London, I went to Leicester.

Of course, I went home at times and was delighted to find that my mother had not been lonely. My friend Annerose had been to visit her, and others, too, had taken her into their homes for coffee and cake, which is an important German tradition. The Lord had truly taken care of her. I learned that the Lord can be trusted for everything.

My time in Leicester was not always easy. As a nurse, being German was sometimes problematic for some patients. One patient told me she would not want an injection from "that blood sucker." The war was not long over, and it was hard for some people to forget. One nurse who was in charge blamed me for anything that went wrong. I shed some tears there, but I also found a very nice friend, Andrea. She invited me to her parents' home for weekends. They, too, were lovely believers. After a year and a half, I took my final exams. Of the eleven students, only five passed, and I was one of them! I could hardly believe it. God had performed another miracle for me. My first reaction was to find a quiet place, kneel down, and thank the Lord.

Missions were still on my mind, so I was advised to do my midwifery training, which would take one more year. So back I went to London, to the Salvation Army hospital in east London. There I met some Dutch girls who also wanted to go to the mission field. They took me to a small Pentecostal church, where I was baptized by immersion. It was a wonderful experience with the Lord. He had clearly spoken to me about it. If Jesus was baptized this way, how much more should I be?

One of the girls, named Corrie, was a very godly woman. She really knew her Bible, so I asked her, "How do you know so much about God's Word?"

She explained that she had been to Bible college in Wales for three years. I began to wonder if I should do the same. I had enjoyed working in London, among the poorest of the poor. The people had hearts of gold. They were ready to share from even the little they had. For sure a cup of tea was always ready, and the midwife got the best cup in the house. I did my practicum in the countryside in the south of England. My bicycle was my mode of transport, with all of my gear stacked in front and behind, even the bedpan. So now I was an RN and a midwife. But again I was thinking about missions. I thought that whatever place I went to, it would also be important to be able to teach God's Word. After all, that is why missionaries go out, to make disciples of all nations as the Lord taught us in Matthew 28:19-20. So off to Bible school I went. My dear mother was in full agreement. And that is where I met my future husband, Teus Kappers.

# 3

# Bible College Life

Studying had never been a strong point for me. Back in Holland, I had studied because I had had to—but now in Bible college I found that I wanted to study. I realized that by studying I could find out more about the love of God and how to apply Scripture to my own life. I also discovered the history of the Bible college I was attending.

The founder of the Bible College of Wales, Rees Howells, was a man of God who lived by faith and who daily practised intercession before the throne of God. His biography, *Rees Howells Intercessor*, is a remarkable story of faith. The college was started in 1924, after the Welsh revival of 1904. Some of the staff had been saved during this revival. They taught us how to live by faith, and their lives were proof of what they were teaching. They had bought the college buildings by faith without having one pound in their pockets. This often made me think of my previous boss and the ravens of Elijah. "God will supply all your need" was their daily slogan—and God did! Outside the main college building was a small monument with the inscription "Jehovah

Jireh" on one side and "Faith is substance" on the other side. I have found it true that the Lord will provide all our needs (but not our wants).

Most of our teachers were retired missionaries or missionaries who had had to return from the field because of circumstances such as wars or illnesses. Most were excellent Bible teachers.

Our daily chores included gardening, painting, baking, and looking after the coal fires that heated the buildings. For the girls, life was a lot harder. They had to scrub floors, wash pots and pans, and help in the kitchen. Maria and her French friend had to take care of the sick and bed-ridden Mrs. Howells, in addition to all their regular duties.

After the second term, we were sent out to local churches which had requested a preacher. I remember the first time I had to preach. I had been given about one week to prepare. Psalm 23 was my chosen topic. When my Dutch friend Harry and I arrived at the church well ahead of time, I felt very intimidated by the size of the building. It was in the heart of Swansea City, and I estimated it could seat well over 1500 people. However, when the service started, there were only twelve people spread around this huge building. The church had seen better days, when the revival had passed through more than sixty years before. My friend, who sat next to me on the pulpit highly elevated above the people, said, "Look. The church is packed." I asked him how he could see those people because I certainly did not. He replied, "The church is full of angels listening and encouraging you."

During my two years in college, I was sent out most Sundays to preach somewhere in south Wales. Many of the chapels in the small villages of the Rhonda Valley were in need of speakers, and I was happy to oblige. This way, I got to practice preaching, and I had to study God's Word in order to prepare. As a side benefit, I met many believers and had fellowship in many homes.

**Forbidden Romance**

College rules were strict. There were to be no conversations or relationships with the opposite sex. In the past, some students had been expelled because of serious violations of this rule. But what do you do when you fall in love? When Maria and I met, we had something in common—our Dutch friend, the missionary in Brazil. I did not dare to tell Maria what this missionary lady had told me. After all, Maria might not be attracted to me. However, I did feel from our first meeting that there was something between us. We were able to talk together at times but always in the presence of other students.

Now it happened that Brother Andrew came for a visit to Swansea University, and I asked special permission to go and meet with him and bring a friend. Permission was given. My choice of friend was Maria because of her interest in Eastern Europe and her interest in the work of Open Doors. We cycled to the university and attended the meeting. We had a great time but had to be back at the college well before supper time because of our duties that evening.

One week later, I asked Maria (by letter) if she would be interested in climbing a local mountain so we could talk a little more about future ministries such as Bible smuggling into the Eastern Bloc countries and also enjoy the beautiful scenery of Swansea Bay. We met halfway and then cycled to the foot of the mountain. The only time I held her hand was on our way down, to help her, as any gentleman would help a lady. But in my heart I knew that she was God's provision for me.

A few days later, I asked Maria to meet me for a secret rendezvous under a giant beech tree on the college grounds, just for a few minutes, as I had an important question to ask her. All lights had to be out by 10:00 p.m., so the arranged time for our meeting was 9.30. It was pouring with rain, "raining cats and dogs" as the Brits would say. We were both wearing long, dark rain clothing, and rain was dripping from our heads. The important question I was there to ask her was: "Maria, will you marry me?" There were no rings, no music, no dinner, just pelting rain. Our commitment to each other was sealed with a warm kiss.

We wanted to be careful not to abuse college rules, and for that reason we kept our distance. We knew of our commitment to each other, and that was enough. Our studies came first, but we did write to each other and sometimes sent gifts of fresh fruit for encouragement.

By December 26, 1971, we were officially engaged in Harderwijk, Holland. When I asked my parents if I could introduce Maria to them, they said yes. I was rather nervous, as Maria was from Germany and Germans were still not that popular in those days as a result of the Second World War. My parents picked us up from Amsterdam airport, but there was little conversation in the car because of the language barrier. I had to do all the translating. Upon our arrival home, my dad told me to get back into the car as he wanted to talk to me man to man. I thought I would now hear their objections and they would send Maria packing. After driving for ten minutes in silence, he stopped the car. He turned to me and said, "Don't you dare dump this girl. If you do, you will not be welcome in our home anymore." What an endorsement! I loved it! Maria became like a daughter to my parents.

Time flew by. In June 1972, our college studies were finished, and we were ready to take on the world—or so we thought. We planned our wedding for September 1, 1972. During the summer holidays, we were able to spend time with Maria's mother and her friends in the Black Forest region of southern Germany. Her mother had suffered much, losing her husband and son and her place of birth. She never saw any of her grandchildren, as she passed away ten months after our wedding.

# 4

# Our Honeymoon

The dictionary says that a honeymoon is "an indefinite period of tenderness and pleasure." Maria and I started our honeymoon on the first of September 1972 after a long, exhausting wedding day with family and guests coming from Germany, France, Ethiopia, Nigeria, Russia, Czechoslovakia, England, and Wales. We had all gathered in the small town of my birth, Harderwijk, Netherlands, where Maria and I were united together before the Lord.

Following this, Maria and I, at long last, were on our own in a small hotel in the middle of the forest, just the two of us—or so we thought. Early on the morning of September 2, we were sitting on the edge of our bed praying together (it had been our custom to pray together every morning ever since we had begun dating) when suddenly we heard the flapping of wings. We opened our eyes and saw a perfectly white dove arriving at our window sill. I got up, walked slowly to the open window, and cradled the dove in my hands. It did not seem frightened. Together we stroked it and thanked the

Lord for this wonderful sign He had given us, an assurance that His presence was with us by His Holy Spirit and that we were part of His beloved people. Our experience with the dove also reminded us of the baptism of Jesus when the Holy Spirit descended on Him like a dove and a voice from heaven said, "This is My beloved Son, with whom I am well pleased" (Matthew 3:17). We realized that we were not just two, but three, like that threefold cord in Ecclesiastes 4:12 that could not easily be broken.

The dove also pointed ahead to what would become our life's work. The logo of Lighthouse Harbour Ministries shows a lighthouse with its beacon reaching out to a ship and pointing seafarers to Christ, the Light of the world (John 8:12). We remember that on one of the first ships ever built Noah released a dove, which finally returned with an olive branch in its beak (Genesis 8:10-11). This was the signal that it had become time for Noah and his family to move out of the ark and get on with their tasks of taking care of the earth and multiplying to fill it (Genesis 8:16-17).

Looking back, Maria and I can only say that God was so good in leading us and blessing us and that He is continuing to guide and bless us, even in our old age. This is our "indefinite time of tenderness and pleasure."

# 5

# Our First Year

Deuteronomy 24:5 says, "When a man takes a new wife, he is not to go out with the army nor be assigned any duty; he shall be free at home for one year and shall make his wife whom he has taken happy." I wished that Jewish law would have been applicable to us in 1972. Our first year was a year of turmoil, of us not knowing what to do or where to go.

Maria started nursing, and I got a job at an azalea nursery, but we knew this would only be temporary until the Lord gave us further directions. We moved into a tiny summer cottage for a couple of months and then into a small mansion on the property of Open Doors, which the organization had recently acquired for expansion of its ministry. The leaders wanted someone to live on the property. We stayed there for about four months. During that Christmas season, a very bad flu epidemic swept the country, and Maria had a miscarriage. Both of us were pretty sick for a few weeks.

Then an English couple invited us to move back to the United Kingdom, to a rural village called

Finchampstead, located about an hour east of London not too far from Windsor Castle. John and Brenda Thorn were involved in a work assisting believers in Eastern Europe. John had been already on a number of trips into that area and had seen the suffering of believers under the hand of communism. Bibles were almost impossible to get and in some situations were copied by hand. John asked us if we would drive him around the UK for his speaking engagements about the ministry. In exchange, we could stay in his apartment for free. We eagerly accepted and lived there for about a year.

Four doors away was a little Baptist chapel with a congregation of about twenty people. A previous pastor had complained about noisy children in his meetings and had told the parents not to bring them back, with the result that the chapel became childless, with no future. One night during our prayer meeting, a village gang was disturbing us by banging on the doors and windows. How could we pray like this? So I went outside and, being the biggest man in our group, gripped one of the boys by his collar. I told him, "You can come inside or clear off, but stop being a nuisance." To our surprise, they all came inside. From that day on, many nights these youngsters would come to our flat for tea, coffee, cookies, and talks. So, we shared the gospel message. About forty years later, on a return visit to the village chapel, we were invited to visit the village postmaster. "Do you remember me?" she asked. We did not. She explained, "I was one of the village gang who made a profession of faith and trust in Jesus."

A group of businessmen from London heard of our interest in Eastern Europe and asked us to make a trip to bring Bibles to Romania and Yugoslavia, with all of the expenses paid by them. We were keen, and so on May 1, 1973 we crossed the English Channel to Belgium in a VW camper loaded with Bibles in boxes. These Bibles were not hidden in secret compartments as I had been used to, as the group did not believe in a .007 style of ministry. The Romanian border crossing was notorious for Bible smugglers being caught. A few weeks previously, some ladies had been found out. Their vehicle had been set on fire, and they had landed in jail for a short time and then been sent back home. With this in mind, we were rather nervous and pleaded with the Lord that we would not have the same experience. We slowly pulled up to the gate, where stern-looking armed guards asked us what our business was. Our answer was partly true: "Holiday."

"Open the side door of your car," they commanded. "We want to do an inspection."

One of the guards worked his way into the van, crawling on top of the boxes to look into the top cupboards. He was sitting and kneeling on top of all of the Bibles but never opened any of the boxes. Our time in Romania with the believers there was very precious. We enjoyed hospitality and fellowship we will never forget.

After returning from our trip, we joined an outreach team in Llangollen, south Wales, where there was an annual international song festival. Our team was led by Reg and Grace Tomlinson, and our outreach was especially aimed at the Eastern European choirs from Poland, Romania, Russia, and Bulgaria. A year after this outreach, Reg and Grace received a call to pastor a small church in Alberta, Canada. We were sad to see them go. Worse news came later when we learned that both had been killed by a disgruntled husband who hated the fact that both his wife and his daughter had become believers through Reg's preaching. The wife and daughter were also killed.

After we returned from Wales, we received a call for help from Germany. Maria's mother was in hospital with heart failure. She passed away a few days after we arrived at her home. These were dark days, especially for Maria.

We also knew that we should not stay in Finchampstead, as we needed to be able to provide for a growing family. Maria was expecting our firstborn. We had prayed to the Lord for children — but only on the condition that they would be saved. We promised, "O Lord God, then You can have them for Your service." I do not think that back then we fully understood the implications of our prayer request.

As our apartment in Finchampstead would be too small, we thought of moving back to Swansea, where we had started an outreach to seafarers when we were college students. We almost bought a small row house, and a mortgage was secured if we needed it. But the lady in whose house we were going to live could not move because her own deal to buy another house had fallen through.

"Why, Lord?" we asked. We became desperate and afraid, not knowing where to go or what to do. "Lord," we prayed, "You have plans for us, not to harm us but to bless us. Have You forgotten us?"

Then, out of the blue—or rather, as an answer to prayer—we received a letter from the London City Mission, inviting us to join their staff in a work among the seamen at Tilbury docks. A house/ministry centre and a small wage were provided. I refused the offer at first, but, with Maria's persuasion, I accepted. But before we moved, we were to have one more trial.

The Christmas season arrived, and we planned to go to Holland and be with my family. Because of Maria's pregnancy, we had to have our GP's permission. "No problem," he said, "as long as you see a doctor after Christmas in Holland just to make sure all is well." And so that is what she did, but all was not well. Maria was told that for the survival of mother and baby she had to go immediately to hospital and be in a dark room with no sound. She had signs of preeclampsia. Her blood pressure was dangerously high. She went to the hospital, and there she stayed for the next six weeks. We found out that our medical insurance from the UK would not cover our hospital bills, which would run into the thousands of dollars. Britain had just joined the European Union, but, as we had been warned before leaving England, medical services had not yet been integrated.

"Lord, what do we do now?" we prayed.

When the azalea nursery learned of our situation, I was invited to work there again for as long as I needed to. This would mean that we would be able to join the Dutch medicare system, and so our problem was solved. Once again, we realized that God was in control. It was a time of great trial, but on February 10 Maria gave birth to a healthy baby boy, Markus. He held the record for being the longest baby ever to be born in that hospital.

Our first year and a bit of married life had surely not been easy, but through it all the Lord had kept us and blessed us with His presence. Our wedding text from Jeremiah 32:39 was becoming true: "I will give them one heart and one way, so that they will fear Me always, for their own good and for the good of their children after them."

# 6
# Lighthouse Harbour Ministries

The story of Lighthouse Harbour Ministries (LHM) is exceptional as much as it is miraculous. For many years, a godly group of people had it in their hearts to visit the sailors of the mighty ocean-going vessels that came into the port of Vancouver in British Columbia. Most of them worked quietly and independently of each other but often in conjunction with other missions and ministries. They included Thor Sundvick of the Shantymen Mission and Walter Homlund and Hans Breevoort, who had been visiting seafarers and distributing Scriptures and gospel recordings in many different languages. Gideon member Bill Nelson specialized in visiting ships from the former Soviet Union, encouraged by Bill Hartin and Ted Dierks. Rev. Jeff Dresselhuis of the Christian Reformed Church and Harold Hanna (whose son Ray would later become a board member of LHM and would become senior chaplain in September 2015) also made visiting seafarers a great priority in their ministries. These and many others were led by God to share their faith with the men of the sea. As a result, many sailors were blessed by the Lord as they received His Word and heard the message of hope in Jesus.

## God's Unique Way of Bringing People Together

In 1970, when I was still a student at the Bible College of Wales, I started visiting sailors. I did not know then that these visits to the ships would later become the backbone of our future ministry. After my marriage to Maria in 1972, we received an unexpected letter from the London City Mission (LCM) in the UK. It invited us to join the mission and work among seafarers in the Port of Tilbury. After some hesitation but much prayer, Maria finally said, "Well, we have been praying for a mission to seamen and a home for our first baby!"

So, for the next nine years we brought up our three children there while ministering to thousands of sailors from many nations, but particularly those from East and West Africa, Eastern Europe, and the former Soviet Bloc. The "Lighthouse," as the mission's building was called, became a true oasis in a very depressing town where many world travellers found salvation through the Lord Jesus Christ. This work with LCM proved to be a great blessing, and our travels throughout the UK proved to be a great encouragement, as we found many believers who would join us by supporting the ministry. It was also a time of preparation for what the Lord had in store for our future.

## Why Move to Canada?

During our time in the UK, we got to know other missionaries to seafarers, mainly through the Merchant Navy Christian Fellowship (MNCF). This mission network helped connect sailors to Christian believers in other ports around the world. Correspondence with these missions before the days of the internet had to be done through "snail mail," so information about vessels and crew members could take some time before they reached another port.

One of the men in correspondence with me was Rev. Jeff Dresselhuis in Vancouver. There was a special bond between us as we were both Dutchmen working in the same ministry, and in 1980 Rev. Dresselhuis invited me to visit Vancouver and see the work that was being done there. Leaving Maria and the children behind in Tilbury would not be easy even for the one week I would be away, but the Lord provided the plane ticket, and, with the end of January 1981 fast approaching, my bags were packed and I was feeling the usual anxiety one faces before a long journey.

The Sunday night before I was to leave, I received a phone call from Jeff in Canada explaining that he was not well and would not be able to receive me. What should I do? The plane ticket would be wasted. Maybe God didn't want me to go to Vancouver. These thoughts were swirling around in my mind. A few hours after the phone conversation, some good friends, former medical missionaries to China and Kenya, came to pray with us and to see me off on my journey. Dr. and Mrs. Thompson had been like spiritual parents to us, and they encouraged me to look in my little MNFC directory to see if there were other possible people I could connect with.

I found another Dutch name in the directory and rang him up to ask him if it would be possible to stay with him for a few days. His response was far from hospitable, as he pointed out that one simply doesn't invite oneself to the home of a perfect stranger. There was another name on the list, Captain Bill Rae. Rae explained that I would not be able to stay with him as he and his wife lived in a small retirement home, but he could give me the number of someone else, who was not in the MNCF handbook. So, I phoned Irish-Canadian department store manager Bill Nelson, only to find that there was no one home, and my call went unanswered. It was Sunday afternoon Vancouver time, so I waited until well after 2:00 a.m. my time and tried again. This time, the Nelson family were home. After some discussion with his wife Valerie, Bill agreed to pick me up at the airport and bring me home to stay with his family.

Early the next morning, I left by train for Heathrow Airport. During the journey, I started having doubts, as I began to think about how everything had transpired. The more I thought about it, the gloomier I felt. While sitting in the train, I suddenly decided to get out at the next station and return to Tilbury. Picking up my suitcase from the rack and stepping out of the compartment onto the platform in Rainham train station, I was abruptly confronted with an enormous poster on the wall of the station which read: "Trust in the Lord with all your heart, and do not lean on your own understanding. In all your ways acknowledge Him, and He will make your paths straight" (Proverbs 3:5-6). Back on the train I went, finally reaching my destination at Vancouver Airport, where Bill Nelson was awaiting my arrival.

**One Week in Canada**

During my stay in Vancouver, I was greatly impressed by the hospitality and kindness of the Nelson family, who had taken in a total stranger. Bill put me into contact with a number of other workers, who had been talking and praying about starting a new mission centre for seamen on the North Shore of Vancouver Harbour. I encouraged them in the work they were doing and told them about the little "Lighthouse" at the Tilbury docks in Britain.

I don't know if it was jetlag or spiritual wrestling, but I had a hard time sleeping those nights. Was the Lord really telling me that this city would be our next place of ministry? For the next few nights, I argued with the Lord and reminded Him of all the negative aspects of moving from our beloved Britain to the other side of the world. Yet, God has a way of usually winning these "wrestling matches." When I phoned Maria to tell her what the Lord had been showing me, she, too, was shocked. I did not dare share this with my host family. I just asked them to keep me informed about the mission's progress. In my mind, I knew that for this to happen there would have to be many miracles of confirmation.

## Confirmation

Less than a month after my return to the UK, a letter arrived from the Nelsons in Vancouver. It said that further prayer and discussion with some of the workers involved in ministry to sailors had led them to ask this question: would Maria and I consider coming to Vancouver later in the year to further discuss and pray together about the possibility of helping to start a new mission? The aim would be to set up a seamen's centre on the North Shore to do evangelism and offer Christian hospitality to seafarers. This letter was a direct confirmation for me that the Lord was bringing the two teams together for a purpose. At the end of September 1981, Maria and I flew to Vancouver (in spite of

Maria being terribly ill with the flu), leaving the children behind in the care of a friend.

During our stay in Vancouver, we discussed and prayed with the group about whether to register the newly formed society and about whether or not Maria and I should make the move to Vancouver. Was this "the way of the Lord"?

On a visit to a local North Vancouver Christian book shop, we met store manager Stella Jo Dean. She happened to also be a member of the city council for the city of North Vancouver, and she was very excited about the proposed ministry. Sailors had been to her store, but she said there was no place locally for them to go and rest for a while. "I will pray and fast for this mission to be established," she promised.

## A Year of Frustration and Change

Soon after Maria and I returned home to the UK, the team back in Vancouver decided to register the newly formed mission with the British Columbia government. On October 7, 1981 the Lighthouse Harbour Ministry (LHM) was officially registered, a bank account was opened, and all the necessary legal documents were put in place. When the team received a copy of the document with legal stamps of incorporation, only then did they really feel it was official.

Back in the UK, we shared with my fellow London City Mission workers the possibility that we might soon be leaving. Though they were sad, they promised to pray with us. For a long time after that, not much happened, so Maria and I began to think that perhaps this was all just a dream.

During the first year of LHM's life, disagreements arose among some of the workers, ending in the resignation of first one, then another, and then yet another of the directors. In hindsight, it might be said that these resignations actually allowed the mission to move forward, yet at the time it was certainly very disappointing.

It was almost the end of the time that had been the target of our prayers, one year from the time when LHM had received its registration, when I received a surprise phone call from Vancouver. Retired businessman George Hardy, who was then chair of the Union Gospel Mission (UGM) in Vancouver, had heard about LHM's start-up and thought that that mission could be of help. UGM had opened a townhouse complex in nearby Surrey, B.C. and was in need of a couple to be the on-site Christian counsellors. Would Maria and I be willing to be that couple? Maria and I saw this as a wonderful answer to prayer. We felt that this opportunity would provide us with both a home and a chance to develop the new mission to seafarers through LHM. Within three months of the call, our immigration papers had been filled out, our interviews at the Canadian embassy in London had been completed, and we had passed the necessary medical tests. And so, we said our farewells to our friends in Britain and were on our way to Vancouver, landing on a cold evening on December 29, 1982.

The move to North America had been a huge undertaking, as all of our belongings, as well as thousands of books and Bibles from Open Doors in the Netherlands, had to make the trip as well. The cost of the entire move, including our plane tickets, had been covered in a miraculous way through some cheques that had arrived in the mail. The Lord had confirmed to Maria through Scripture that God would lead us to "a spacious land...where there is no lack of anything" (Judges 18:10).

**All Beginnings Are Difficult**

Our first year in Canada was not particularly easy. Often Maria and I felt that we had made the wrong decision, having left friends in the UK and the stability of the well-organized team at the London City Mission. It was also not easy for our three children to settle into a new culture and a new school system.

We soon realized that our role as Christian "counsellors" simply was not working out as originally planned, and we received a new title as "managers" for the housing complex instead. In practice, this meant they we had to be "jacks of all trades," unplugging toilets, settling disputes among the tenants, and doing whatever else had to be done.

After fulfilling our one-year commitment at the complex, we moved to North Burnaby to be closer to the ships.

There were, however, some great encouragements. We had started a prayer group with people who were getting involved in visiting ships. During one of these prayer meetings, three people in attendance informed the group that the little church they attended was closing down and the church building was going to be sold. They felt strongly that the Lord was leading them to give half of the proceeds to LHM for the purchase of a building to be used as a seamen's centre. What an encouragement it was when $75,000 was donated for the project! It was, and still is, evident that God's work will never lack God's supply.

During those early months, some new board members joined LHM, including retired department store manager Dale Wallace, businessman Bill Hartin, and itinerant preacher and author John Williams. All were respected members of the local Christian community who already had leadership responsibilities with local churches and other organizations. These men proved to be a tremendous help in building a solid foundation for the mission.

### Searching for a Building

As funds began to come in, the board felt it was a good time to start looking for a suitable building near the waterfront—only to discover that municipal bylaws would not allow us to use any of the proposed sites. But North Vancouver city councillor Stella Jo Dean had promised to help LHM get an amendment to the bylaws passed which would allow the mission to get the necessary permits. It was thought that the legal processes, including at least two public hearings at city hall, might take a year. A suitable building was found opposite North Vancouver's dry dock at 260 East Esplanade. An offer of $110,000 was made and accepted, but more funds would be needed for renovations. Yet again, God's supply was never lacking, and soon even the needed furniture was provided.

In due course, the new "Lighthouse" was ready to receive the first sailors. However, the mission received legal notice from the strata council of the complex where the building was located objecting to having a seamen's mission on the site. The strata council believed it would create a "hooker area," an environment where prostitution would flourish, which would be detrimental to the community. Some of the LHM board members thought the building should be sold in favour of buying another in a new location. However, both Maria and I felt strongly that this site was God's choice and that LHM should commit the situation to prayer. Prayer partners around the world were contacted to intercede for a change of heart among the strata council members. At the final council meeting, there was a miraculous change in attitude, and, after some safety issues were discussed, the council agreed to allow the centre to open, with its first day of operation set for Christmas Day, 1985. Ironically, the council member who had accused the mission of creating a "hooker area" opened an office for "call girls" and "escorts" right next door to the centre! After we prayed against this spiritual attack, however, city hall became aware of the situation, and the office was shut down after a few weeks.

**Volunteers and Staff**

In order for the centre to be staffed sufficiently, a small army of volunteers was needed to both visit the ships and serve the sailors who came to the centre, sharing the love of Jesus with them. The "Lord of the Harvest" blessed LHM with many willing workers, beginning with the appointment of Thor Sundvick as the first director for the centre in North Vancouver. Most of the volunteer staff had never met any seafarers before joining, and the language barriers that existed because of the multitude of nationalities that were represented on board ships could be a big challenge. The use of Christian films, especially the Campus Crusade *Jesus* film, and a large selection of foreign language Christian literature were key components to communicating the gospel to these seafarers from a multitude of nations.

For over three decades, hundreds of volunteers have been able to minister to sailors from all over the world and in so doing have themselves been recipients of great blessing. Thousands of amazing stories and testimonies from these unique encounters have been shared throughout the years and could fill many volumes. From the very beginning, it has always been the central aim of LHM that the gospel of Jesus Christ would be made known. The gospel is the power of God for salvation, and it is this message that has changed the lives of thousands of men with whom LHM volunteers have prayed and shared. While the mission does not keep any official records of these encounters and decisions made, their names are undoubtedly written in the Lamb's Book of Life (Revelation 20:12).

## A Volunteer's Story

Reg and Sissi Bullet came from the UK and had only recently arrived in Vancouver when they decided they would like to volunteer at the Lighthouse. Reg had been in the British army during the Second World War. He had been imprisoned by the Japanese in Hong Kong and later taken to the infamous labour camp that built a bridge over the River Kwai. When he had been liberated at the end of the war, he had been not much more than a walking skeleton, and it was a miracle he had even survived. Terrible memories still haunted him of the abuse he had received from both Japanese and Korean guards in the camp. He shared with Maria and me that even though he had forgiven his tormentors as Christ had forgiven him, he was afraid of how he might react if he was confronted by Japanese or Korean sailors. Together we prayed that the Lord would give him grace to love those sailors if the situation arose. As God would have it, the very first sailors to come through the door on his first shift at the Lighthouse were from Korea. God was good and powerfully at work in the lives of our volunteers. As it turned out, the Korean sailors were fellow believers looking for fellowship with other Christians, and Reg and Sissi spent the afternoon sharing and praying with these brothers in Christ.

## A Vision for New Ministries around British Columbia

Since the 1980s, Vancouver Missions Fest has had a huge impact on the local Christian community. For a few days each year in late January, Christian organizations such as LHM have been able to exhibit their ministries at trade and convention centres and other large venues. It was at the second of these events that John and Sue Woelke come over from Nanaimo, B.C. on Vancouver Island to see how God might want them to be involved in some kind of mission service. John was a retired businessman, and Sue had been a school teacher on a Native reserve. As they were walking through the aisles between the mission booths, Sue accidentally tripped over an electrical wire. She stumbled right into the arms of LHM volunteer Ken Chitty, who was manning the LHM booth together with his wife June. "Now that I've caught you, I'd like to tell you what the ministry of LHM is all about!" Ken exclaimed. This was the beginning of Lighthouse Harbour Ministry Nanaimo.

Another place Maria and I became interested in was the port of Prince Rupert, along the northwest coast of B.C. close to Alaska. After some time in prayer, it was decided that I would fly there and spend a weekend with church leaders and other interested parties. At first, it seemed as if this was going to be an immediate success, as a small group of ship visitors was established. Later that year, Ken and June Chitty spent a month in the port training the new workers in the details of ministering to seamen. It was therefore very disappointing when, a few months later, the group fell apart. It seemed as though all that time, money, and effort had been spent for nothing. But things would eventually turn around. A number of years later, in the summer of 2007, Neal Friesen contacted LHM. He and his wife Elfrieda had moved from Toronto to Prince Rupert to be closer to their sons. As they had settled into the community, the many freighters in the port and the sailors wandering around the small town had not escaped their notice. Some friends remembered LHM's past involvement in the port and provided

Neal with contact details. "Can you come over and help us?" Neal asked. Encouraged by such a surprising turn of events, Maria and I flew out to Prince Rupert shortly afterwards to help the Friesens and a new team make a fresh start. Today, an active independent group of workers runs the Prince Rupert Lighthouse Harbour Ministry, and their seamen's centre in town provides a welcome home away from home for "those who go down to the sea in ships" (Psalm 107:23). In 2013, Pastor Zito, a full-time chaplain from the Philippines, was hired to take on the role of leading the work in Prince Rupert.

**Cruise Ship Ministry**

The average freighter these days has about 22 crew members on board, down from about 45 when we started the ministry in 1970. Cruise ships, however, are a different story. As these huge liners increase in size, so does the need for crew members to serve the passengers. The largest cruise ship today has space for more than six thousand passengers and over three thousand crew. From April until October, many cruise ships call in at the ports of Vancouver and Victoria and sail to different destinations in Alaska and the Pacific Northwest. The spiritual needs of these crew members have not been overlooked, and Maria and I made an attempt some years ago to start an LHM outreach specifically to the multi-ethnic men and women

64

who work on these floating palaces. For two years, we rented a small office at the Vancouver waterfront.

With the closure of this terminal, the ministry had to look elsewhere. Victoria, B.C. appeared to be another port where we could do this ministry. Victoria was an up and coming harbour for cruise ships sailing between Seattle and a variety of Alaskan ports. Once again, for two years LHM rented an office at the terminal. However, because of port personnel changes and because of personal health reasons, LHM was unable to rent the office again.

We continued to struggle to find volunteers willing to serve at a place near the ships. A letter was sent to each evangelical church in Victoria without any result. While Maria and I felt that we could not travel and oversee another ministry, the vision never left us. Finally, Pastor Dennis Scott volunteered to be the chair of a newly formed ministry to the cruise ships in Victoria. For one year, Maria and I worked from the back of our van parked at the terminal, contacting the crews, giving out Christian literature and the *Jesus* DVD in 32 languages, and sometimes praying with crew members before they went back to their ship to work.

A breakthrough came in the spring of 2012 when the Port Authority permitted the mission to put up a marquee-sized tent next to the Port

Authority's, right next to where the cruise ships came in to dock at the terminal. The location could not have been better, and a full-time chaplain, retired South African Navy officer Cecil Kleu, was hired. Now thousands of seafarers come to the Lighthouse tent to use the WiFi in order to contact their families. In 2015, Victoria Lighthouse Ministry was registered as an independent mission. The port authorities have been very pleased and expect this to be a long-term arrangement. Thousands of Bibles, New Testaments, books, and DVDs have been given out for free and taken around the world, to be read and looked at not only by the crew members but also by their families and friends.

### Fraser Surrey Docks

Facing another "giant" was unusual for me. I don't encounter many men matching my six-foot, seven-inch frame. However, as Maria and I walked into the office of the CEO of the Fraser River Port Authority (now called Fraser Vancouver Port Authority), I could not help but smile and comment, "I know where you get your clothing." This exchange immediately broke the ice, and Maria and I were able to present to him the work of LHM.

The Fraser Surrey Docks are a multi-purpose port located on the Fraser River just south of Vancouver and host a fair number of ships. Some of the vessels bring in steel, and others take on raw lumber. Usually these ships stay in port for at least a few days, unlike container ships, which stay in port for no more than a day or so. Even the Port Authority had thought it would be good for a seamen's mission to be there. How timely this visit was! The port had three trailers they would sell to the mission, and the port would also lease a piece of land to LHM for a dollar per year. After much prayer and discussion, the LHM board decided to go ahead with the project. With much volunteer labour and hard work, the three 30-by-30-foot trailers were put together, and a very presentable new Lighthouse Seamen's Centre was opened in the spring of 1996. This centre would stay under the direct responsibility of Vancouver LHM.

I remember one of the first seaman coming into the place one evening. I showed him the *Jesus* film, which he watched with great interest. Near the end of the movie, when Jesus is crucified and the sky grows dark, a real earthquake shook the building at its foundations, causing some things to fall off the shelves. The frightened seaman asked me, "How did you do that?" Of course, I had done nothing, but it was a perfectly timed rumbling, warning all of us in our province of British Columbia that "a larger earthquake is overdue."

This centre on the Fraser River has been operating for many years and now has a new team of volunteers serving there.

The events of 9/11 were a huge game changer for seafarers and missions around the world.

Previously, we could just drive into a port and walk onto the ships. That all changed for security reasons. High fences, photo permits, and other security checks are now normal for all mission workers in order to get onto the ships, as well as for the sailors to get shore leave. Some Russian sailors joked with us and said: "It is worse here than in the former Soviet Union!" Because of the changes in port security, sailors wanting to get to any of the centres have to walk many miles, sometimes through rain and snow and in the dark. LHM, therefore, decided to purchase two vans and hire drivers to drive the seafarers from ship to centre. Two vans and two drivers are a large annual expense, but here also the Lord was in control. Besides driving, the new staff also could witness to the seamen.

Around 2008, the Fraser River Port authorities suggested we move our location to somewhere nearer the main gate. After some time, they came up with our present site, but they required us to build something new while buying back the old trailers. After a generous gift of $80,000 was given to LHM for the purpose of building this new centre, the team knew that God was in it. Architectural drawings were made and approved by the authorities, and more gifts started to come in. LHM agreed to set a starting date for June 2008. A retired but not so tired builder, Dan Reimer, had challenged us to build most of the building with volunteer workers. This would cut the cost in half, and so about a dozen able men under Dan's leadership, volunteers willing to listen, learn, and get blisters on their hands, started working on the foundation. Six months later, on December 1, the old centre was closed, and a beautiful West Coast style building was opened. Maria enjoyed doing the interior design and provided luncheons for the hard-working men. By the time of completion, no money was left, but none was needed as the project had used the exact amount budgeted.

**More Workers Needed**

In the early 1990s, as LHM started to grow, more staff were needed. Our office manager was going to retire, and a search for a replacement started. The amount of administration required had gone beyond what could be done by volunteers, and we were in need of a full-time chaplain/ administrator. It was felt that the person should also spend at least one day a week visiting seafarers so as not to spend his entire time in the office but also have the experience of doing evangelism. This would also help him in his correspondence with supporters.

Paul Ratsoy was God's choice for the job. His background was in banking, but he had felt for some time that he wanted to do more work for the Kingdom of God. As his vision for the LHM ministry grew, he wrote some very practical Bible study books especially geared to seafarers who had little or no knowledge of the Word of God. This ministry has proved to be very fruitful, as many sailors have completed these Bible studies. Another area of ministry where God has used Paul is to Muslim sailors, who come from countries which are normally closed to the gospel. Often, encounters with a chaplain like Paul may be the only time these Muslim sailors have an opportunity to meet and discuss the Bible with a Christian.

Some of the most difficult seafarers to reach with the gospel in the 1970s were the Chinese. At that time, none of them was ever willing to accept any piece of Christian literature or even have a conversation. I remember an encounter I had at the Lighthouse in Tilbury, UK. A group of about twelve men, all dressed in the same drab, blue clothing, were walking outside our home. As none spoke any English, I motioned them to come into our home, and to my surprise they did. They were curious as they looked into many of our cupboards and even our bedroom. Maria motioned them to sit down and indicated that she would make them some *chah* (tea). They nodded, and within a few minutes she had produced twelve mugs of tea and cookies. Our triumph was short lived, however. They discovered some Christian Chinese language literature, which made them all immediately stand up and leave our home, not having touched the tea or cookies. Today, however, things have changed a great deal. Cracks have started to appear in the communist system, and a whole people group who had been at one time the most closed to the gospel have become the most open to God's Word. Many have put their faith in the Lord Jesus Christ, as has been happening with the Chinese diaspora in other parts of the world.

A Chinese church in Vancouver invited me to preach to their young people, and it was there that I was introduced to William and Mona Lam. They were originally from Mainland China but had moved to Hong Kong and later on to Canada. Their desire to reach their own people was very obvious, and after they had spent time with other Chinese volunteers (Bill Pen and David Wong) visiting ships and volunteering in our centres, it became obvious that God had called them to LHM to oversee the Chinese ministry. William's business experience has proved to be of great help within LHM. Mona has been a great influence, as she often directs the men in spiritual worship in the evenings.

The work and ministry of LHM could never have been done without a tireless small army of volunteers who spend many months visiting ships, running the centres, knitting toques for seamen, and baking cookies. The many financial supporters who have trusted the mission with their gifts to the Lord will undoubtedly see eternal results. When we look back over the years of God's faithfulness in supplying all of the mission's needs, the contributions and donations have totaled into the many millions. Hundreds of thousands of sailors have made the Lighthouse their home away from home, and tons of literature, Bibles, Gospels, and other books have been freely distributed to seamen and taken back to their homes for their families to read. Our hope and prayer is that this testimony and story will have inspired others with a longing to be used by God just as He has used LHM. Perhaps God wants them to be involved with LHM in one way or another, or maybe He wants them to serve somewhere else in the world. As Christians, it is our responsibility to fulfill the Great Commission at the place where God puts us, glorifying Him, until He comes or calls us home.

# 7
# A Letter from a Seaman

Some time back, our Lighthouse Seamen's Centre in Vancouver received the following letter:

*Good day, sirs.*

*Peace and grace to you from our Lord Jesus Christ.*

*I am sending my thanks and appreciation to Lighthouse Seamen's Centre in Vancouver.*

*I was a seaman officer who many times called in at the Port of Vancouver on the vessels MV Copilco, MV Amity Ace, MV Azlan, MV Emerald 10, and many more. Back in 1991, during our discharging and loading at Vancouver, somebody visited our ship and give us a New Testament and other tracts. Through frequent reading of the Word of God, I was saved and accepted the Lord Jesus Christ as my personal Saviour. I become a member of the Baptist Christian Church in the Philippines.*

*But it is not easy to be a Christian. I had an accident on our ship that would force me to retire early (in 2002). At first, I did not realize that God was calling me to be a missionary pastor. I spent five years in Bible school, and, by the Grace of God, I am presently working as a missionary pastor in the province of Cavite, Philippines.*

*I found your address in the New Testament you gave me. That's why I'm sending you this letter to express my gratitude for your priceless mission to seafarers. For God's glory, you've accomplished Christ's Great Commission (Matthew 28:19-20, Mark 16:15).*

*On behalf of our church, we will always pray for your ministry to seamen.*

*Many thanks again, and God bless you all.*

*Benny*

*Benedicto I. Cruz*
*Saving Grace Gospel Ministries*
*Freedomville Evangelism Centre*
*Naic, Cavite, Philippines*

# 8
# At the Edge of Hell

"I can't kill anymore," cried the man we had met just a few minutes before.

It happened some years ago when the telephone rang just as we were getting into bed. I looked at the alarm clock, and it showed 11.55 p.m. We thought it might be a relative from Europe who had forgotten the time difference. Maria encouraged me to pick up the phone, which I did.

A deep voice on the other end of the line said, "Come to the airport."

"Who are you?" I asked. "And what do you want at this time of the night?"

His answer came in the German language, so I quickly handed the phone to Maria. After a short conversation, she said, "Yes, we will come."

It was a strange experience, to say the least. We arrived at the Vancouver Airport at about 1:00 a.m., which was totally deserted except for some cleaners. Arnold (not his real name) sat at the curbside just in front of the main entrance. When he stood up, he did look like Arnold Schwarzenegger, all muscle. We wondered what we had gotten ourselves into.

We sat down at a small table inside the terminal, and then we asked Arnold to tell us his story. We could see that he was very burdened, and we wondered why he had called us at this unearthly hour.

His first words were: "I cannot kill anymore."

Well, that made us feel a little better! He then told us his life story. He had grown up in a small German village and at a young age had joined the village gang. From then on, his life had become even more exciting as he first got involved in the drug trade and then enlisted in the French Foreign Legion.

"They taught me how to kill," he said. "I have killed many innocent people, but now I cannot do that anymore. I feel so guilty. Can you help me? I need an answer for my life."

We told him that the only one who could help him was Jesus.

On hearing the name of Jesus, he went ballistic and slammed his fist onto the table so hard that we thought it would split in two. He screamed, "You have come to me to tell me this nonsense? Do you know that I can kill you in two seconds?"

My heart sank, and the only thing I could think was, "Why on earth did we leave our cozy beds and come here to talk with this evil lunatic?"

But Maria, undeterred, fired back at him, saying calmly, "No, you cannot kill us. Jesus is stronger than you." For the next hour or so, she explained the gospel to him. He sputtered from time to time, but she said, "You called us. You asked for help, and so now is your time to listen."

At the end of our long conversation, we prayed with him and gave him a Mariner's New Testament, but it seemed as if Arnold had hardened his heart.

Now, many years later, we still wonder what happened to him. Is he still alive? He was on route to Hong Kong to commit his next contract killing. We warned him that he was at the edge of hell. The seed was planted, but we suppose that only eternity will reveal what happened to Arnold.

# 9
# Happy But Still in Prison

Although I had not yet been on the MV Espirito Santo (Holy Spirit), because of its unusual name I was excited about what the Lord had in store for me on this ship. Once aboard, I met a very gloomy looking captain. "Can I be of any help to you today? I am from the Lighthouse Seamen's Centre," I said.

"No, you cannot," he abruptly answered.

"What's wrong then? If you don't tell me, for sure I cannot help you," I responded.

Speaking in Portuguese , the captain then gave orders to an officer, who took me mid-ship. There, he unbolted the door to a heavy metal enclosure and asked, "You are sure you want to help?"

There is a saying that "Curiosity kills the cat." I am not a cat, but I was curious. However, I became a bit scared when the officer pushed me into a dark area and bolted the door behind me. In complete darkness, I sensed the presence of other bodies in a very stinky place, and I could hear another language being spoken. I discovered I was sharing the space with four African stowaways, who had sneaked onto the ship in Mombassa, Kenya. Possessing little hope for a positive future, they had taken the potentially life-ending risk of illegally boarding a ship.

With stowaways aboard, the ship's reception in various ports, including Vancouver, would be very poor, and the stowaways' future looked bleak indeed. But what could I do? I was only a missionary! Before leaving the ship, I promised the men and the ship's captain that I would make a phone call on behalf of the fugitives. Although I was happy to depart the ship and return to Canadian soil, I also wanted to keep my promise. I called an immigration lawyer, who was keen to hear my story. In the end, a few minutes before the ship was to sail for Brazil, the four Africans were escorted off the ship by police and sent to a local prison. Amazingly, however, everyone was happy!

Later, I went to see the four former stowaways in order to share the gospel with them. When we met, I was very surprised to see four incredibly happy fellows. They had never had it so good in their lives, they said. They could choose what to eat, whether to read the newspaper or watch television, etc. (This is prison Canadian style.)

I put a damper on the joy of these four very grateful men by saying, "You may be free and happy, but you are still in prison."

I reflected afterward that the story of the stowaways is similar to the lives of many people who are very comfortable but still remain prisoners of sin. John 8:36 promises: "So if the Son [that is, Jesus] sets you free, you really will be free."

# 10
# From Costco to Christ

Shopping is not my favourite pastime, maybe with a few exceptions such as going to a well-organized garden centre or flower shop because they remind me of Holland and home. Another exception is going to Costco. After all, there are many "man toys" there, plus all the free tastings. I have never tried to go a second time past a tasting table, for fear the lady there would say, "You have already had your share." At the end of our shopping expedition, Maria and I usually reward ourselves with a Costco lunch.

One day, there was a man sitting alone at the table next to us, the same man who had sat there the last time we had been there, and the time before that. I remembered him because of his longish, gray, curly hair. He probably also remembered me, and we smiled at each other as Maria and I sat down. I became curious when I noticed a little notebook in front of him. He looked as if he might be a Costco employee, as he was taking notes from time to time. So, I asked him if he worked for Costco.

With a big smile, he said, "Oh, no. I work the stock market."

I had always thought that stock market traders would wear suits and ties, but he wasn't.

"I use my phone for making my transactions," he said.

I did not want to look stupid and pretended to know at least a little about his field of work. "Do you do most of your trading on the TSX or Nasdac or the Vancouver Stock Exchange?" I asked.

"Wherever I can make money," he answered.

Wanting to sound clever, I asked him if there was going to be a stock market crash this September, as there had been seven years earlier and again seven years before that.

"How do you know that?" he asked.

"I don't know," I said, "but I have read newspaper articles and listened to Warren Buffet about market crashes."

"How do you make money?" he asked.

"Well, I don't," I answered.

"How then do you live?" he asked, obviously puzzled.

I told him that my Father is very rich, I ask Him, and He looks after me very well.

This must have sounded very attractive to him, and after a few moments of silence he asked, "Do you think your father would adopt me?"

Maria, who had been silent up to that moment, responded with great enthusiasm, "Sure, He will. We are also adopted by Him."

It took us a little while to explain our lives to him. We told him that we had become followers of Jesus Christ and that after that our heavenly Father had looked after us for many years.

I don't know if the stock markets closed up or down that day, but our friend left us still with a big smile on his face. Maybe we will see him again on our next Costco visit.

What a privilege to have been adopted by our heavenly Father (Ephesians 1:5) and to know that we can call on Him any time we have a need!

# 11
# Some Final Words

Christians talk about "walking with the Lord."
But it takes time to learn how to do it—and how to
keep doing it.

The Scripture text at our wedding was that "A
threefold cord is not quickly broken" (Ecclesiastes
4:12 NKJV). We have tasted and seen that "all the
promises of God in Him [Jesus] are Yes, and in Him
Amen, to the glory of God" (2 Corinthians 1:20
NKJV)—as long as we keep walking with Him. The
old hymn says, "Trust and obey, for there's no other
way to be happy in Jesus, but to trust and obey." The
hymn also says, "When we walk with the Lord in
the light of His Word, what a glory He sheds on our
way." Maria and I have seen Him at work in many
miraculous ways. We have learned that God is so
good—all the time! One day, we will see the fullness
of His glory, and we will be with Him. Oh, what a
day that will be—and it will last for all eternity!

Can we ask you? Have you put your trust in the
Lord Jesus Christ? If not, you can start your walk
with Him today by trusting and accepting His work
of salvation for you. He loves you so much and

showed that by dying on the cross for your sin, to set you free from the bondage of darkness.

The work of Lighthouse Harbour Ministries could never have been done without a tireless army of volunteers and the many financial supporters who have trusted the mission with their gifts to the Lord. If God wants you to be involved with LHM in one way or another, please contact the mission at:

Unit 1, 260 East Esplanade
North Vancouver, B.C., Canada V7L 1A3
Phone: 604-988-5084
E-mail: info@sealight.org
Website: www.sealight.org

CPSIA information can be obtained
at www.ICGtesting.com
Printed in the USA
BVHW030808081222
653664BV00007B/147

9 781777 192624